IMPENDING RECESSION:

How to Escape 9-5 Rat Race to Follow Your Dream

SAJID INAYAT

TABLE OF CONTENTS:

DISCLAIMER:

The advice provided in this material is general advice only. It has been prepared without taking into account your objectives, financial situation or needs. Before acting on this advice you should consider the appropriateness of the advice, having regard to your own objectives, financial situation, and needs. Where quoted, past performance is not indicative of future performance.

The author and the publisher of this book disclaims all and any guarantees, undertakings and warranties, expressed or implied, and shall not be liable for any loss or damage whatsoever (including human or computer error, negligent or otherwise, or incidental or consequential loss or damage) arising out of or in connection with any use or reliance on the information or advice on this site. The user must accept sole responsibility associated with the use of this material, irrespective of the purpose for which such use or results are applied. The information in this material is no substitute for financial advice.

HOW TO QUICKLY SWITCH FROM AN EMPLOYEE TO AN ENTREPRENEURIAL MINDSET

The most dangerous way of living life in the monetary society is relying on a single source of income and fixed hourly wage.

You can learn every single possible way of making money in bullish and bearish market conditions and still fail to make money. Every year, for over three centuries, men and women are graduating from prestigious universities where top experts are teaching them everything there is to know about micro and macro economy and finances and yet, only a handful turn into millionaires.

How do you explain that disappointing fact?

Simple. A wrong mindset that ultimately failed to go through the necessary change.

Unfortunately, that same mindset is common for the majority of the global population. And that's the main reason why only two percent of people own eighty percent of everything this planet has to offer and why measly one percent hold forty-six percent of all the money in the world.

For them, terms such as *income* and *fixed* don't exist because they are being constantly reminded of one life-important fact: **for as long as your income is *fixed*, there's a not-so-high upper limit designed to keep you in line and ruthlessly controlled.**

Most commonly, a fixed income is connected with a single source of income otherwise known as the 9-5 job. However, in that context, even working two or three jobs is still considered a single source of income that is paid fixed.

As you are well aware, it is often claimed that hard work is what it takes to build a fortune. How many men and women do you personally know that work two jobs and still have difficulties meeting the ends?

They clearly don't lack determination. They are not shying away from labor either. So how come they can't move from the ground zero or even worse, debt?

Because they have what is known as the *employee mentality* or *employee mindset*.

And now, we are going to make that crucial switch.

Necessary initial psychological triggers (dangers of your current lifestyle)

An *employee mindset* is something deeply rooted in any individual. It is a direct consequence of years of entirely wrong tutoring.

You see, the largest part of the population -- and that most likely includes you -- had been raised to believe that the only way to live a life is to finish school, find a job and stick with it. Sounds familiar?

In 2009, after the crash of the global financial markets, we saw thousands of men and women who were regularly making six and even seven figures a year setting tents on the parking lots across the country. All of them made this same tragic mistake: **blindly believing in a single source of income and fixed hourly wage upon which they based their entire lives**. It took just a few months of a negative trend for their "systems" to collapse.

Unlike them, those with an *entrepreneurial mindset* immediately seized a plethora of opportunities to not only make money but to multiply it by flipping houses, starting cleaning businesses, lending money on high interest, etc. They went through the otherwise dreadful and devastating situation untouched and by the time the recession ended, the world has seen a rapid increase in the number of millionaires worldwide.

ALL THANKS TO THE MAJOR SHIFT IN A WAY THEY PERCEIVE OUR MODERN MONETARY-MARKET SYSTEM

For them, it's the best system mankind has ever built.

Unlike the older societal setups where a central figure such as king controlled every aspect of people's lives, this new one enables equal chances for everyone. In other words, you don't have to be a member of the aristocracy to build yourself a fortune; something unseen and rather impossible only two hundred fifty years ago. And we have the *institute of debt* to thank for that unlikely opportunity.

Here's the problem.

To an *employee*, debt is something connected with anxiety, fear, stress, heavy burden, and downfall. The term itself is associated with everything wrong and negative with this society. And to some extent, that's logical and justified reasoning because if you don't understand the true purpose of *debt*, you can't see the forest from the tree.

In reality, it is *debt* that allows us to pull a trick on Mother Nature and its notion of *survival of the fittest*.

Unlike the wildlife that is destined to slow and agonizing death when the environment cannot support them any longer, human beings can not only survive but also thrive in the worst possible conditions. A young lion cub exposed to a severe scarcity of food sources will inevitably cease to exist. Thanks to *debt,* a young human being can ever start from the point of a negative balance - as many do. Before we even set our foot on the path of independence, the majority of us are already paying back student loans, for example.

Unfortunately, due to the lack of proper tutoring or the total absence of one, many perceive those same student loans as a *burden* and it's exactly that entirely wrong perception that defines the *employee mindset*.

In the *entrepreneurial* mind, on the other hand, that loan is an advantage and not a burden because it allows acquiring the most important survival skill (a rather expensive knowledge) without any need to earn money beforehand. A simple signature on the piece of paper is enough to set us on the growth trajectory path simply because we the humans enabled such a great option for ourselves.

How do we make money in the monetary-market society?

Through market exchange where we are trading value for value. In other words, we are selling.

For an entrepreneur, that value is either some service or product. For an employee, however, that value is physical or intellectual labor. An entrepreneur is free to make an unlimited number of exchanges with an entire world - some seven point four billion people at this moment. An employee, on the other hand, can only make the exchange with a single person or entity – an employer.

When an entrepreneur is exchanging values, there's no limit. Nothing is *fixed*. And that's something out of reach for every single employee in the world because as the rule of thumb, an employee *earns* money by selling labor at the highest possible price per hour of labor he or she was able to negotiate with an employer. Sadly, in most cases, that hourly wage is hanging on the minimum we require to survive.

And what do we do when things go south and it becomes painfully clear that we won't be able to pay our next rent due in a few days? We loan money with interest consequently degrading the quality of our lives because push has already come to shove only we failed to react on time. Without us even realizing, our micro monetary system went in recession followed by the deepest depression we've ever experienced before.

That's something that can never happen to an *entrepreneurial mindset* and that's why you must make the switch as soon as possible. But for that to occur, you'll need something more than just an initial trigger.

You'll need the **motivation** to persevere.

Main drives of a complete transformation

Do you know what happens the morning after you quit your 9-5 and after spending years inside the "Matrix"?

You jump up from the bed before the dawn, all sweaty and with heart pumping like you just ran a marathon when your brain finally realizes that there's no paycheck coming any time soon or ever again for that matter. You suddenly feel exposed and vulnerable like an addict going through rehab. All those years of "comfortable" life where someone else was taking care of a few capital aspects of your existence for you (read: the boss) turned you into an addict that craves for the next shot.

Sure, the wage wasn't something to brag about in the public but at least you didn't have to worry about things like marketing, sales, finances, etc.. You do your required duties (that you negotiated with your employer the day you signed the contract) and every two weeks some nice lady in accounting sends your pre-agreed fixed income to your bank account.

But that morning, the nice lady is nowhere to be seen. There's nobody but you to ensure that money is regularly arriving on your account. A wave of heat surges through your body at that moment and you find yourself completely awake. You don't even need the usual shot of caffeine to get you going. The anxiety is keeping you on the edge.

And that's perfectly fine. It's exactly how you're supposed to feel because now, for the first time in your life, you feel the real **need**.

That *need* is the most powerful motivator because if we don't *need* it, we won't put the best of our efforts into it. In other words, **if you want to get motivated about your dream, then quit**. Create the need to create motivation. That's all that is to it.

Sounds too radical?

Read the following sentence, please:

"I *have to* go to the store to pick groceries."

It's a common thought or statement you are using every day. However, just a swift analysis shows that the *action* (going to the store and picking up groceries) has not been well-defined. It's vague, doesn't have a precise deadline, can or doesn't have to be done at all.

Now read this one:

"I **must** go to the store to pick groceries."

When you say it to someone, the first thought that comes to mind is, "Oh, the guests are coming" or "Those supplies are seriously deflated." Even in that other person's mind, the sentence creates a sense of emergency. It has to be done right away or else.

Here's the real kicker.

The *I have to go* statement is a classic employee mindset. Sure, yeah, it would be great to make more money but I already have a job and receiving regular paychecks so no rush. I can spend a few more years daydreaming.

At the same time, the *I must go* statement is a standard entrepreneur. If I don't make it work, no money will come any time soon and I'll end up in a dire situation. So I better move like now or else!

You feel the thirst immediately after you realize that there's no water flowing through the pipes. Even if you had a glass right before it happened, your brain creates an instant need to force you into action. But for as long as there's pipe water coming out, you're fine. And that's basic human nature.

As mammals, we are lazy by default. Give us food, water, some roof over our heads, air to breathe and if possible a few good sexual encounters a month and we're good. Our brains are simply wired to keep us alive using minimal resources possible. Just try to run and do some more complex math like multiplying 112x13 and you'll immediately notice how you're instinctively slowing down. In fact, to solve that mathematical problem, you'll come to a full stop. The same is true with puzzling questions. The more mental energy it requires, the sooner we are giving up entirely.

But not the *entrepreneurial mindset*.

That brain is working overtime to solve problems daily. It quickly comes to the point where it turns into a way of life. When there's no problem to solve, the anxiety is rising. Something just doesn't feel right.

So, to sum up, if you are determined to escape the 9-5 rat race, the first thing you need to do is to **create the need**.

In other words, your dream must get the main propulsion drive installed or it will remain just this cute idea that's been swirling through your mind. And as time goes by, the dream will eventually fade away because your primary mammal nature will kick in and permanently seal you inside the deadly Matrix.

The first step in that mission is changing three principal habits.

Changing the habits

Jim Rohn, a late motivational speaker and business coach, once said that **every person is the sum of five people he or she is spending the most time with**. So take a good look around. What do you see? Do you see successful individuals that seem unstoppable? Do you feel motivated in their vicinity, just by listening to them talking?

I'm willing to place a good bet that it isn't the case.

A FORBIDDEN HABIT

First, let's see if we could break the code and see what lies beneath that entire deal, OK? Because, Jim's right, you know.

Without you even realizing, by the time you reached the age of twelve, your central belief system or the set of principles upon which you are living life has been completely formed. And you can thank one specific survival mechanism for that.

According to Athene's research in the field of neuroscience and basic human behavior, as a human, you are living in a state of constant duality between how you see yourself and how others are seeing you. Therefore, for you to survive and thrive in your closest social and physical environment, your expressions must meet acceptance. If, however, they get rejected, you are immediately falling in a state of acute depression. The rejection inhibits the serotonin release, a vital neurotransmitter responsible for feeling good about yourself, to put it in simple words. Serotonin is also known as the *leadership chemical* because even the people around you can feel the kick in your brain. The more powerful it is, the more likely is the scenario where you are perceived as their leader.

How can something like this happen?

What's happening to your body and mind when you are watching your favorite team kicking ass on the field?

Thanks to *mirror neurons*, you are capable of experiencing a third-party's action as your own. In other words, you feel both their joy when they are winning and sadness and grief when they are losing. By the way, that's the reason why so many people end up hooked on pornography because sex is the single most powerful drive. When you are watching an erotic or pornographic scene, your brain is releasing exactly the same mixture of chemicals as it would in the real event where you are the main protagonist.

It's these mirror neurons that allow us to perfectly blend in our closest social and physical environment as the precursor to our survival. This is one of the most primordial mechanisms we possess and as you will soon learn, its influence on our lives is immense.

So let's take your close group of friends for example.

The only reason you are having a good time with them is your almost unnatural ability to adjust to your environment. If you stick out for any number of reasons, and under the assumption that you're not a perceived leader of the group, you'll end up marginalized and eventually ghosted and dumped.

Now, I want you to take a sheet of paper and on the left side, write five names. Five people you're spending the most time with. And on the right side, write the five "traits." Like this:

Name 1	*Justifies*
Name 2	*Blames*
Name 3	*Envies*
Name 4	*Defeatist*
Name 5	*Lazy*

Think hard about each of your people. Look deep inside their souls. Connect the name with a specific trait. It's OK if you don't "use" all the traits. Who knows, perhaps you are surrounded with just blamers and justifiers.

Alright, what does it mean?

If one of your friends has a tendency to start his arguments and sentences in general with: *"If it wasn't for _____; then I would've _____,"* you are dealing with a **justifier**.

This type of person can even find an excuse for not taking out the trash.

"I don't know, man, I think I would be successful if only my folks were able to afford Harvard."

And then you go, "How about that Howard Shultz? The guy dropped out of school when he was just sixteen and look at him now. And he grew up in some really bad neighborhood. "

Of course, you refrain from saying that out loud because you are a sensible person who wouldn't like to hurt someone's feelings. Well, just so we're clear, every time your friend *justifies*, he's not just offending you and everyone around but he's also doing something much worse – he is actively dragging you down with him. Remember, you are adjusting to fit in the group.

Moving on...

"I would bring home more money, dammit, but those corrupt asses are taking everything."

"It's not my fault that the paycheck is puny. All the money goes to that one percent of one percent."

Hearing that a lot from someone within your group? That's a **blamer**. Always someone to blame for own "misfortune" as they like to describe it.

Is it really "misfortune"?

If you step in a dog's poop on your way home, it's A) not a dog's fault, B) not a dog owner's fault, and, finally, C) not an unlucky incident. You willingly stepped at that exact spot.

Why willingly?

Because unlike the seed you picked up with your right shoe the last time you took a stroll through the park that fell right in front of a moving vehicle just to end up crashed, you are a being that is perfectly capable of choosing your direction.

In other words, the seed didn't have any choice. It could've fallen off the tree and grow on the spot, could've been blown a couple of yards north or end up stuck on someone's shoe. That's just the way that organism evolved, that's all. That poor seed that is now just a speck of dust on the street was not *unlucky* by any definition.

Nor were you when you stepped in poop for that matter. You were simply reckless or completely disinterested in the world around you.

Again, your *blamer* friend is slowly drowning you whether you're realizing it or not.

OK. Let's dissect the next guy...

Let me start by saying that I really do hope that you are not hanging around with someone who openly **envies** everyone and everything.

These people are the bottom of the barrel if you ask me because they will make every effort to drag you down – even if it means backstabbing in both abstract and literal way.

The reason why they are willing to hurt someone is that they could feel better about themselves. You know, *if my cow drops dead, I hope the neighbor's drops dead too* policy.

I believe they are in a state of ecstasy now with this global lockdown caused by the coronavirus. The people they are envying the most, and, by the way, those are the folks closest to them, are now in the same pickle they are. Deep inside they are hoping that their "nemeses" will lose their jobs and incomes altogether so they could finally gloat.

Seriously, if you can find even a trace of envy in any of your "friends," either move away or block that person entirely. He or she is the poison that's been eating you away. It's only a matter of time before you fall.

But now comes that guy. We all have one of those. We all know the type. If it's someone too close to us, like a parent; then the impact becomes far more dangerous.

We are talking about **defeatists** or the people who mark even the simplest things as something impossible to achieve or make. The fact that we landed on the Moon back in 1969 using a funny technology from today's perspective, doesn't seem to have any effect on them.

In 2014, Ryan Grepper came up with an idea to improve one of the dullest gadgets ever. Up until then, portable coolers were these passive plastic boxes, often too large or too impractical to carry around. But they did their purpose. However, Ryan thought of a neat way to make this dull piece of plastic interesting to young people. He imagined adding music, some lights, and USB ports to them, plus, equipping them with things like plates and glasses so you'd have a small portable picnic party inside a single easy-to-handle box.

"I don't know, Ryan...in this economy? Are you sure? Remember Mike and how he..."

Long story short, Ryan Grapper ultimately raised almost $14 million via crowdfunding in less than a month. And while he was adjusting to being a millionaire, that friend of his, who made every effort to discourage him from turning his dream into reality, is probably searching for coins inside the chairs.

Here's the thing with defeatists and all of those who tend to use the word *impossible* all too often: they are afraid; plain and simple.

By marking something *impossible*, they are justifying their reluctance to even try. But to live with themselves, they will use every opportunity to knock another person off the track. And they will do that in the most ridiculous way possible like drawing a parallel between your idea and the current situation on the Chinese financial market.

You will often hear that friend of yours using financial jargon and terms like *recession, Dow, bearish, crash, stagnation, fed rates,* and alike. At the same time, that person is making a living doing something that has nothing to do with financial markets, but that doesn't seem to bear any significance.

If that guy was Ryan's father, and it might just be the case, then he turns from a *defeatist* into something much worse. He becomes a *dream-crusher*.

A person of immense influence who is repeatedly telling you that you cannot succeed in something you dream of will either ignite defiance in you or crush your spirit. Unfortunately, the latter is more common.

Finally, there's a guy or a gal who prefers spending days in front of the TV doing nothing or, in the best-case scenario, playing games or going out. And for that, he or she needs you. Don't get me wrong, games are fun but do try to assess the time you are spending watching meaningless TV shows, playing games, and hanging in a bar. Does the sum of these activities leave you enough time to pursue your dream?

The main lesson here? Ditch every person you can identify as any of these five. That's the first habit you need to change to succeed in virtually anything. Build an impenetrable wall between you and all those who justify, envy, blame and then extend on defeatists and lazy asses. Surround yourself with people that inspire you and push you forward instead. In fact, it's better to be alone than to have someone dragging you down every chance he or she gets.

That's the first habit. Now comes the really important one.

A MILLIONAIRE'S WAY WITH MONEY

2% of people own 80% of everything this planet has to offer. 1% of people hold 46% of all the money we have in the system.

How these statements make you feel? Do you believe that this tiny minority is responsible for everything that is wrong with this world?

Let's check this out from another angle.

Two percent of people is some 150,000,000 men and women. That's almost half of the USA. Not that "tiny" after all, is it?

Did you know that every 11th household in America hides a millionaire? Every time you step outside and turn right or left, you are inevitably passing by a millionaire's home. How's that for a fact of life?

Half of that number, some 75,000,000 people are considered the richest on the planet. Again, not a small number. There are entire countries that are nowhere near that number of residents. Could they all be part of the same deviant group that is plotting against the rest of the world? Of course, not.

These are simply the folks who figured out the secret and that secret is something we mentioned at the beginning of the book: it's the money that turns ordinary people into millionaires and millionaires into billionaires. It's not hard work or time management as some claim. The whole trick is using the money you made in the past in the same way you are using your arms, legs, and sweat at your job.

In retrospect, that means that you failed to become a millionaire thus far due to poor money management skills. For you, money is something that has taken almost an unnatural form. For you and the majority of people, money is the prize. And that's not what money is.

Money is sweat. I want you to remember that.

Money is merely a tool, a mean to an end. And that end -- the prize -- is a lavish lifestyle where you can drop by some fancy restaurant at any time and order a dish (that bears the name you can't even understand) without looking at the right side of the menu.

The prize is living like a king and without a single worry on your mind because the money you made in the past is now making new money. In other words, while you are shooting golf balls from the deck of your 100-foot yacht that is slowly drifting in the middle of the Mediterranean, you don't have to think about the bills because there's someone taking care of that for you.

However, to reach that moment, we have to correct one serious flaw in your matrix.

How often were you witnessing your parents arguing about money and bills while you were just a child?

Remember what we said about the central belief system? It's completely formed by the age of twelve and it's practically the sum of the expressions coming from your closest social and physical environment.

That is to say that, your young brain was learning from the environment and adjusting your actions and responses accordingly. So if you were exposed to scenes in which your father is getting a mouthful from your mother because the money's been scarce, you grew to resent money. Because in every dispute or argument, money was that thing that seemed to be the cause of it.

So now, when you are fully grown and making your own living, you are perceiving money more like a nemesis than a friend.

And since nobody taught you how to manage it, money is this strange thing you know you need but don't really know how to handle it. For all intents and purposes, the money you are making is only good for purchasing food, paying utilities, mortgage or rent, and buying things you don't even need. All that time, you've been missing on the true purpose of money.

That true purpose or the reason why an ordinary guy turns into a millionaire seemingly overnight is

INVESTING.

Just like you are using your brain, arms, legs, torso, and sweat to get the job done so you'd receive your paycheck every second Friday, that guy is using money to make money. He is *investing* the portion of the money he made by selling his labor for a fixed hourly wage in a hope that one day, his investment portfolio will start yielding returns. And lo and behold, it did just that even sooner than he thought it would be possible.

But before he was able to invest even a dime of his hard-earned money, he had to adjust the way he was managing that money.

So he made a simple money management plan:

- 40% of everything he makes is for current spending
- 50% goes into an investment portfolio
- 5% goes to reserves for rainy days
- 5% goes to personal education

Now, you might be wondering how it's even possible to survive with only forty percent of what you make every month.

That's the big secret right there.

Remember when we talked about creating a need to become motivated and determined?

This guy created a need simply by allocating 60% of every dime he makes to things outside the current spending. By staying stubborn about it, he was quickly forced to come up with more money because it's obvious that 40% won't cut it. And thus, he kicked the snowball.

One thing led to another until eventually, he reached the point of sync with the system or the point where the money you made in past is now making new money at an accelerated rate without your direct influence. And it took less than three years to achieve that level of comfort.

So when do you start?

NOW! Get everything you have and split it 50/50 for now. It's about developing a habit vital for your future success because, as P. T. Barnum concludes in his bible of wealth, only 20% of all the money you make -- one way or another -- is yours to spend.

Billionaires are, therefore, those people who reached the point where they are using less than 10% of everything they make for their own extremely lavish needs.

The bottom line is, if there's one habit you need on your future journey toward millions and success, that's proper money management and this is the single best way of handling your money to build wealth in the shortest time possible. It is the only way.

Remember Grepper? The guy with Coolest Cooler™ idea? The man raised almost $14 million from the crowd (the money he doesn't even have to return) but due to the poor money management, five years into the project, everything shut down. Only half of the supporters received their portable parties while the other part can kiss their money goodbye since Grepper recently filed for Chapter 11, effectively shutting down the company.

It's like this: **if I give you a jet right now would you be able to fly it?**

Exactly! Now, why on Earth would someone be confident enough to suddenly manage millions when he or she didn't develop a habit of managing a few hundred dollars first?

That's why you don't "wait until you save a couple of thousands before investing" but start splitting the money immediately even if it's only a buck. It's about developing a good habit before anything else. The habit that creates an instant need overnight. After all, the investment game is all about proper money management.

In normal or bullish market conditions, that game is easy. But when things go south and strong bearish trend takes over, the rules of engagement change slightly. Those prepared thrive. Others die.

PREPARING FOR THE UPCOMING MARKET CRASH

The first thing you need to do is to catch the signals on time because once in recession, those who were too late are having a hard time catching up on the train.

Recognizing the signals before anyone else

At 00:58:53 UTC, on December 26, 2004, a massive rupture along the fault between Burma and the Indian tectonic plates caused a devastating undersea earthquake followed by the mega-tsunami that killed approx. 230,000 people.

Nobody could predict what was about to happen immediately after the ground finally stopped shaking. However, minutes before the first wave hit the coastline, animals had already fled to the higher ground. They could sense that something ominous is rolling over the sea.

The same way animals can sense the upcoming environmental danger, so can we predict the destabilization of our system. After all, we built it. The mechanisms that drive the monetary-market system are designed by us; therefore, it is relatively easy to notice a rupture that will most likely trigger a tsunami and leave tens of thousands exposed.

One potential indicator of the soon-to-happen negative trend is:

INCREASE IN DIVORCES RATES

It seems that, just like animals, women can sense the looming threat because, by the time markets respond to the negative circumstances, women start ditching their men at the accelerated rate.

That's how it all starts. Companies in particular sectors are the first to experience the negative impact of the change caused by any number of events on a micro or macro scale. The very first thing they do to hedge against the risk is to immediately lower the wages. When that fails, people start losing their jobs. Consequently, the family budget depletes and divorce suddenly becomes a viable option.

So, as trivial as it may seem, if you notice an uptick in the number of divorcees, start running simulations because something bad is most likely rolling over the hill.

Another thing you should keep monitoring comes from the least known source available to everyone.

SHORTING

How many ads have you seen so far inviting you to make money on Forex or Binary options?

Well, if you sign up at any of these exchanges, you will gain immediate access to a plethora of different analytical tools and analyses that are built for only one purpose - to help you invest smartly.

One of these indicators is the *buy/sell* **ratio in a total corpus of investors for a specific option**.

The game works fairly simple. If you believe that the option, say some commodity, stock, bond, index or base currency in a currency pair will go up in value, you execute a *buy* option. If your analyses showed a potential for a sudden downtrend, you'll execute a *sell* option. You are basically betting on the future trend of a specific option. That's all to it.

On December 17, 2017, a cryptocurrency Bitcoin hit its maximum historical price, $19,783.21. Before that moment, the majority of positions were long, meaning that most investors were executing a *buy* option. However, immediately after BTC reached its peak, the market sentiment turned against it. Investors' patience reached a critical point and the trend suddenly shifted. Everybody started selling which eventually caused the price to plunge below $5,000 in one-year time.

Now, here's the important thing.

If you notice this behavior on a massive scale; then you are most likely too late. True, it will just confirm that something is happening with the markets and that imminent downtrend on a global scale is inevitable. However, to be on the safe side, you should keep an eye on different options at all times just to see if some significant index is showing signs of illness BEFORE the outbreak of massive hysteria.

For example, once the Bitcoin bubble burst, it took all cryptocurrencies down with it due to its perceived status of some virtual gold.

This event immediately reflected in several markets and industries because a lot of money was invested at the beginning of the process (inflating the bubble). The dramatic downfall affected every single market even indirectly connected to blockchain in general. Granted, global consequences were avoided since blockchain and cryptocurrencies are still making a very small part in the overall financial system but still, it's a good example of how a trend of a single option can end catastrophically. Most importantly, it demonstrates a simple-to-understand analytical method that may indicate serious turmoil.

However, this method has its limits. Remember that. While you can access technical, fundamental, and sentiment analyses, you can't see behind the curtain. In other words, you are unable to see what well-known so-called, *big shorters* are doing.

These are the people who specialize in "betting" against the option(s). And they are usually first to notice that something is off because they are placing their full focus on bad news.

With that being said, monitoring global shorting, when used in conjunction with the rest of the methods we'll explain here, will give you heads up beforehand.

The next signal comes from the *game of cocks*.

TRADE WARS

When Donald Trump announced that the government will increase tariffs on imports from China, what happened? All major indices plummeted.

Trade wars are extreme market movers and in some instances can even cause the downtrend on global financial markets when two major players collide.

However, on its own, a trade war can't trigger the crash or recession. But it can add fuel to the fire and cause potential long-lasting consequences if conditions are right. And it's also just one way governments affect the global economy.

Another one is:

QUANTITATIVE EASING (MARKET MANIPULATION)

Every time you hear this seemingly complex financial term, you immediately know that something is wrong. Quantitative easing is nothing more than a government's buyout of the so-called, "toxic assets" that banks accumulated over time in a hope of restoring the markets.

It does sound rather helpful but it can backfire. It's the move that has only one purpose: market manipulation that will, hopefully, stir things up and restart the beast. It eventually does that but it usually takes time for the effect to show. Meantime, people suffer the consequences.

Here's an example. When something happens that could potentially threaten the banking sector, like the real estate market crash of 2008, banks are immediately locking their money. In other words, they stop loaning to small businesses that, while commonly perceived risky, are the usual customers. As a consequence, small businesses are prevented from expanding and even normal functioning which results in layoffs. And small businesses are responsible for employing over 60% of the total US workforce.

To counter this, the central bank starts lowering the rates. If you've been following at least some news from the financial sector, you've been hearing a lot about "fed rates."

This decrease turns the attention of the banking sector toward government-issued bonds. They want to use the money they hold to capitalize on the difference (buying at 0% or 0.25% interest and selling at 2-2.5% interest; thus, making 0.75-2.5% profit).

In reality, the government simply tricks the banks to release the money. So now when all that money is in the government's hands, they are slowly pumping it back into the banking sector through the buyout of toxic assets which are nothing more than worthless options since the secondary market that is supposed to trade these options no longer exists. For example, stocks of the companies that are about to default.

Banks feel sudden relief and that's when fed rates start rising again. This forces banks to turn to their primary market – small business owners since government bonds are rendered invaluable due to the increase in rates. At that moment, the only way to make a profit is to loan money at high interest to the commercial market.

We've seen this mechanism in action back in the 2008/09 crisis. And so we know that it can take years before we experience positive results of such market manipulation. Nevertheless, it's worth knowing that the moment somebody mentions *quantitative easing*, you know that something's off.

MAJOR GEOPOLITICAL TURMOIL, WAR OR TERROR ATTACKS

Contrary to general belief, wars positively affect markets. They trigger domestic production on a massive scale. But only if they are localized and on foreign soil.

The same cannot be said for major geopolitical turmoil because it induces an unhealthy level of fear. As a result, investors are abandoning virtual assets (i.e. stocks) and acquiring commodities (i.e. gold). This well-known psychology of the herd is causing rapid downfall across the financial markets and if the situation continues to escalate over a longer period, it can cause a crash and even recession.

Lately, geopolitical turmoil often generates a terror attack. On September 11, 2001, America came to a standstill. For two weeks, the country's borders were of the limits. Nothing went in or out. As dreadful as it was, the 9/11 attack shows how markets react to such an event. The same happened in London in 2005.

People are sensitive about their investment portfolios and it doesn't take much for the sentiment to change. The sense of fear induced by a single devastating event affects the decision-making process and forces people to make irrational moves. The fact that since 1926, markets were in positive trends 74% of the time bears none of the importance during the crisis.

And that *crisis* is usually caused by the #1 cause of the market crash:

THE BUBBLE

Keep adding the air and it will eventually burst. That's the rule of the bubble. Unfortunately, we love to do it only instead of air, we are commonly using *derivatives*. It's just a simplified way to describe *unreasonable confidence* and any *lack of common sense*.

By definition, a *derivative* is an arrangement or instrument whose value derives from and is dependent on the value of an underlying asset.

You probably heard about Deutsche Bank, right? Well, IMF claims that Deutsche Bank is the single most dangerous threat to the global economy. In case you missed the news, DB is the bank with $49 trillion in exposure to derivatives.

What are *derivatives* in simple words, you ask?

Say your neighbor owns a large orchard. And one day, the two of us start talking about the future of his business. Somewhere along the line, we decide to place the bet on whether his almond business will thrive or default. Others overhear us and they too decide to join the action.

However, none of us has the money to cover our bets. So instead, we're using only 2-10% of our own money while "borrowing" the rest at high interest or even with leverage. And the game goes on until one summer, a drought on an unimaginable scale hits our region and destroys every single orchard in a wider area. The almond business that is in the center of our bets defaults. That's when the bet is due and that's when everybody realizes that nobody has the money to pay the bet.

Something similar happened back in 2006. If you watched Adam McKay's Big Short, you've seen how these derivatives in the housing market (subprime mortgages) triggered an avalanche that ultimately caused the global economy to fall in a recession two years later. And, in case you are unaware, subprimes are making a comeback only now, they are called *nonprime mortgages*.

Now, bubbles are relatively easy to spot. Usually, whenever there's too much hype around some idea (i.e. subprime mortgages, Bitcoin and cryptocurrencies in general, dot-com revolution back in the 90s), but that hype has no solid foundations, you are looking at the bubble that keeps receiving air. The 2008 crash was caused by short-sighted bankers who were only interested in making quick cash knowing that if things go south, taxpayers will cover their debt. And that's exactly what happened.

Last but not least...

UNKNOWN UNKNOWNS

Former Secretary of Defense, Donald Rumsfeld, wrote the following in his response to a question about the lack of evidence that link the Iraqi government with the weapons of mass destruction:

> *"Reports that say that something hasn't happened are always interesting to me because as we know, there are known knowns; there are things we know we know. We also know there are known unknowns; that is to say, we know there are some things we do not know. But there are also unknown unknowns—the ones we don't know we don't know. And if one looks throughout the history of our country and other free countries, it is the latter category that tends to be the difficult ones."*

On December 30, 2019, 7.4 billion people across the world went to sleep completely unaware that somewhere in China, a few people developed unusual pneumonia. By the time the western world woke up, China has already alarmed WHO about the potential outbreak of some new, potentially fast-spreading decease.

Still, nobody was too worried about it. It was something happening far away. Until it spilled over the Chinese borders and spread across the world.

Coronavirus or COVID-19, given its global impact, is effectively one of those *unknown unknowns* Mr. Rumsfeld wrote about. A microscopic organism nobody could predict is now slowly but surely leading the world's economies into a disaster. Financial markets are responding to the outbreak in an anticipated way; investors are fleeing, trying to exchange virtual assets for precious metals. Indices are in a steady downtrend in all major markets. The crash now seems unavoidable.

But can we also talk about the *recession*? How likely is the coronavirus outbreak to cause something like that?

Conditions leading to a complete crash and recession

Quite often, you are hearing the terms *recession;* or *bear market*; or *market crash,* or even *depression*. But do you understand them? Can you distinguish one from another?

When markets are going through a negative trend, three points in the declining curve indicate the possibility of the recession:

1. CORRECTION (10% decline)
2. BEAR MARKET (20% decline)
3. **MARKET CRASH** (30-60% decline)

But we are still not in a recession. For that to happen, the negative trend must continue for at least three (3) consecutive months. That's when it's safe to say that the world or a country is in *recession*. Although, some financial experts are using six (6) months as the reference point.

If the recession extends to a period of minimum one (1) year – or two (2) according to some – with a parallel decline in GDP by 10%; then we are in *depression*.

It sounds rather dreadful but the truth is you can make millions even during the darkest times if you prepare on time.

8-Step preparation protocol

In our world, there's only one
rule: is my violence greater
than yours.

When you war-game a certain situation, you radically increase your chances of success. In the scenario where the world's economies are crashing down under the burden of their ignorance and lack of better judgment, those prepared are cashing in.

But to do that effectively, they have to breach through personal moral boundaries because, as you will soon see, capitalizing in recession often involves the exploitation of the fellow human's misery.

The first thing you need to do as part of your preparations is obvious:

1. PREDICTING THE EVENT

So far, we have a relatively good run with markets. They are (more or less) up for eleven consecutive years. That's a long period by anyone's standard. But what goes up must come down eventually.

In this step, however, it's not important to predict the exact moment. This is more about being psychologically prepared for the event so that panic, which will spread across the universe, doesn't affect your decision-making process.

2. CASH SUPPLIES

This is where the statement from the beginning mostly applies.

The majority will be forced to sell for pennies on the dollar. While it may sound unethical to capitalize on someone else's misery, that's exactly what you need to do. Because, "The time to buy is when there's blood in the streets," as Baron Rothschild once said.

The last recession destroyed homeowners. At the same time, their situation provided a fertile ground for real estate investors with cash. They were able to buy at almost ridiculous prices and then sell afterward when the market stabilized.

That's the deal here. You are making a medium-term investment by buying some collectible that usually sells for a couple of millions for a fraction of that just to sell in 3, 5, 10 years later when it bounces back.

3. STEER AWAY FROM MAJOR (REAL ESTATE) CONTRACTS

Prices are still too high. In times of recession, you wait for the blood to start flowing down the street before you take out your wallet.

In such conditions, no industry or market passes untouched and undamaged. So whatever is that you are eyeing, think twice before you put your money in it.

4. AGE TOLERANCE ASSESSMENT

It takes time for the markets to restore and for the game to pick up on the pace. Usually, it's some 5-7 years before pieces come back together. Your age is a determining factor in any kind of long-term investment or immediate response.

That is to say that, a young(er) person can afford a much higher risk because there are still years ahead to recover even from a complete loss. An older generation, however, shouldn't feel so free to gamble with their assets. A wrong decision could turn out to be deadly.

5. SHIFT TO PRECIOUS METALS

Gold never loses its luster. In times of recession, when money is scarce and virtual options are rendered worthless at least for the time being, precious metals are one of those commodities that not only hold but also increase their value.

If you've been following financial news for some time now, you've noticed how gold markets respond to a short-term crisis. On even the slightest news of trouble, investors are clearing the parts of their options' portfolios to make room for gold. That's the moment when the price of gold moves up.

And when the crush becomes inevitable, gold quickly proves why it's "precious."

6. CASH IN THE PERCENTAGE OF YOUR PROFITS

This is directly related to the second step. You need cash and the quickest way to obtain some of it is to cash in on a part of your profits. Some investors are even selling their properties BEFORE the markets hit the lows just to have enough money to steer through tough times.

Which leads us to our next step:

7. RE-ASSESS YOUR PORTFOLIO

Take a step back and see how exposed you are. Every portfolio includes at least some risk exposure. Mostly, we are talking about derivatives so now would be a good time to get rid of those because they are the first thing that will sustain the hit when things go south.

8. BECOME AN EXPERT IN WHAT YOU DO

Making yourself irreplaceable is the name of the game here if you are pursuing a career of some kind. In dire times, low-level employees that haven't still proved their worth are the first to go. Only those who are considered experts in their fields remain.

As you've already learned, the first response in the times of crisis is layoffs. And the first names that end up on the list are a) newcomers, b) non-productive employees, and, finally, c) least skillful ones.

Now when you are prepared, it's time to make money.

MAKING MILLIONS IN RECESSION

It's not business as usual. During the recession, people are more sensitive. An average income drops down. The unemployment rate suddenly spikes. There's less cash flowing through the system because everybody's on the edge and refraining from excessive spending.

Still, people are buying. Life just must go on. Today more than ever. And that's where you come in.

3 principal business strategies

Whatever you choose as your monetization method(s), there are three main strategies you should use in these times. They perfectly respond to the circumstances, making you highly adjustable to the new market conditions.

CAPITALIZING ON UNCERTAINTY

In other words, sense from where the fear is coming and then capitalize on the perceived weakness. We are talking about your clients, opponents, suppliers, and everybody involved.

In times of recession, there's one thing we have in abundance and that's fear. You simply can't miss it. All parties in the process, in your industry and/or niche, are afraid of something. So when you take a step back and look deep, can you see the source of that fear? More importantly, can you somehow capitalize on it?

It sounds rather ominous and even borderline corrupt, but it's not, because most money is made by exploiting some sort of fear.

For example, crime rates rise during dire times. Breaking and entries, car thefts, frauds, etc. As you can imagine, two industries are making the most out of the situation and that's surveillance and security and insurance industries.

EXPLOITING THE UNPREPARED AND OVERCONFIDENT

The majority will be caught by surprise. That will make it easier to break through their defense.

Of course, we are not just talking about potential customers but also competitors because some of them will simply be overconfident and let their guard down. That fact presents with the good opportunity to push in their usual market which, under the normal circumstances, would be out of reach for you.

PROVIDING COMFORT

This is more of a long-term strategy where you'll secure the customer base by literally stealing them away from your overconfident, unprepared or damaged competitors.

Eventually, the situation will normalize and you'll emerge from the whole situation even stronger than you've been.

The good (although risky) example is buying off retirement funds from senior citizens at half the price or even buying off debt and then offering to freeze clients' obligations for an extended period until markets resume their formal glory. You are perceived as a savior and nothing can beat that image.

Whenever the people are anxious and on the edge, the best business is selling comfort. Remember that.

6 smartest logistical steps

To execute any of the above-explained strategies, you'll need to build a solid foundation. And the first thing you must pay special attention to is:

1. PERSONALIZED NETWORKING

You can talk to a person or with the person. The difference is huge.

By getting closer to your customers, on a more personal level, you are deepening the relationship, ensuring that nothing and no one can stand between you and a person or entity that buys from you. In times of uncertainty, having someone you can trust is a commodity. Keep that in mind when communicating with your customers.

2. ADJUSTING YOUR STORY

Your brand's communication in the event of the recession has to follow the same premise explained above. Messages should become more personal. For example, if we are talking about the brand, share insights and show people behind the scene. Let your market know that there are men and women with their personal stories and fears working overtime to create for or deliver to them.

The bottom line is that your brand should appear warm and sensible and not cold and distant as it will be the case with the majority of your competitors. Most importantly, double down on the frequency of broadcasting such messages.

3. TUNE-UP THE DISTRACTION ELEMENT

Again, this is only building upon the previous two where you'll use distraction to shift their minds from problems and negativity. A nervous, agitated, anxious or afraid prospect is no buyer. Your communication must be perceived as the safe haven, sort of a relief bubble where they feel shielded from the potentially deadly outside elements.

This is an important step in high-power branding where, in troubled times, a brand is taking an almost supernatural shape and serve as the refuge for all those that feel rejected. Let this soak for a moment...

To achieve all of this, you need to prep everything beforehand and that means "upgrading" your team so they would be able to respond most efficiently.

4. SUPPLY YOUR TEAM WITH PLAYBOOK

Consider the fact that the majority of your team members (be it traditional or remote) don't know how to steer through tough times. They need guidance. But instead of wasting your time on day-to-day tutoring, create an array of instructional guides and put it all inside a simple-to-use playbook.

That way, every single member will know how to respond in any given circumstance. And remember, in recession, things mostly work against you. Especially if you have a half-prepared team.

5. TEAM-UP WITH A RELIABLE PARTNER(S)

Going through unknown woods in the night can prove itself dangerous. You may accidentally trip. But by aligning with a like-minded partner, you are hedging against that risk because now there are two, three or even five and more individuals determined to make it regardless of the situation.

It's like having a trust of brains all working for the same agenda.

If you take a swift look in the 2008/09 crisis, you'll notice how smart micro and small businesses partnered to endure through tough times. On their own, they didn't stand a chance. By merging, however, they were more flexible to respond to the challenges.

Another reason why you should consider a partnership, especially if you're going to use online channels, is to extend your inventory. Most small entrepreneurs fail to realize that having a limited inventory doesn't provide enough "energy" to compete in a volatile or troubling time. This is also true in normal market conditions.

6. TRIM YOUR PORTFOLIO

Meet John. John owns 18 properties, has stakes in twenty-something businesses, sits in a dozen different boards. Don't be like John because John's head is about to explode when things go south. He will have too much on his mind to focus on what's important.

The point is to trim down as much as you can so you'd reduce distraction and operate from a more comfortable position.

Alright, now when we've built a solid foundation, it's time to learn the top ways to make money in the recession and even depression if it comes to that.

The classic that never fails

Franchising. Acquiring a done-for-you business with an established brand. It can be anything at all that fits the situation but it will depend on the amount of money you are willing to invest.

NOW, WHY PEOPLE CHOOSE FRANCHISING IN THE FIRST PLACE?

First, you don't have to spend time and money to build a new brand from the ground up. Second, your business is coming with a manual which is not the case when you are starting from scratch.

However…

Just because some food or service franchise comes with a manual, it doesn't necessarily mean that it's a walk through the park. In most cases, you are buying a license. It's up to you to build the infrastructure.

But here's the deal with franchises: the more you invest, the less manual labor you have to put into it.

For example, franchises that go from $200K to $1M and more, come fully equipped. You are landing on the executive level. As the price goes down, level or your direct engagement goes up. That is to say that, if you buy a service franchise like some cleaning or delivering business at $10K or $20K, you are investing your labor to cover for the low price.

At the same time, and this is important to remember, buying from a reseller that used to run a franchise business at the fraction of the price, doesn't necessarily have to be a good deal. It's more likely that the business wasn't going well and now a guy is selling for pennies on the dollar just to save what can be saved.

HOW DO YOU CHOOSE THE BEST FRANCHISE?

It depends on your personal preferences and circumstances. For example, in the current situation (COVID-19-related limitations), food delivery businesses are booming. Across the world, restaurants closed their doors while people are asked and, in some instances, ordered to stay indoors. It doesn't take a genius to figure out how well they are cashing in right now.

Back in the 2008/09 crisis, cleaning service franchises were some of the most profitable businesses because all those foreclosed properties required a thorough cleansing before banks and real estate investors could resell them. We are most likely to see a similar scenario because thousands have already lost their jobs so they won't be able to keep up with mortgages.

Again, it's about merging a personal interest, a situation, and a budget.

2 proven money-making methods suitable for anyone

Neither requires you to even exit your front door. Today, thousands of entrepreneurs are making millions from their home offices and living rooms by handling every single part of the business via the internet. But two methods simply stand out.

YOUTUBE

In its essence, the game is simple: you keep rolling out quality content and then cash in either on AdSense or through direct sales or both. And we are talking about six and seven figures annually, net.

However, there's a catch.

First of all, you need a minimum of one good video a week; otherwise, people will forget you. If you could publish more in a single week, that would be great.

Second, there is no compromise when it comes to quality.

Now, the obvious problem with this method is the equipment, personal skills, and an immense amount of time that you need to invest. If nothing else, we can be honest and say that not everybody is suitable to appear on the screen. So if that's not your thing, and you can't fit in some kind of animated illustration with voiceover, you might want to consider the Option #2.

SOCIAL MEDIA MARKETING

We are not talking about starting an agency here. I mean, you might consider that option but if you don't have a healthy level of experience in the field, it would be like teaching someone how to drive a car while not knowing yourself.

However, you don't have to be an expert to use social media as your main sales channel. After all, 4 billion people connect to the internet daily and 98% of them spend time on social networks. Even better, 50% or some two billion buy stuff online. In most of the cases, their decision-making process is influenced by a well-crafted social media marketing campaign and sales pitches.

There's only one rule you need to remember:

You need to pick only one social network in the beginning.

To be able to make the right pick, there are three additional rules of engagement you need to consider.

Number one: **where are your people?**

Every social network has its own culture. It is; therefore, suitable for a specific group of people. For example, a hardcore Redditor will hardly ever use Instagram. A younger person is more likely to respond to an Instagram post while the older Millennials and Gen X are easier to reach on Facebook. If visual is something that fits your future business, Pinterest might be the best option.

Here's the rhetorical question: should you first pick your product/service or a specific demographic? What is the right order of things here?

There is none. Some online entrepreneurs prefer flexibility, meaning that they are moving from one demographic to another according to the demand for something they can acquire with ease. Others stay devoted to a single audience and never deviate. Whether they pick the product first and then search for the right demographic or vice versa, they are never exiting their comfort zone. So once again, it all comes down to personal preferences.

Number two: **you have to appear before them**.

And that "appearance" must leave a positive impression time after time. Plus, you don't want to come out too pushy especially in the beginning while you are still building your flock.

So, whatever social network you choose, you must adjust your appearance accordingly to blend in the culture. Deviate from this simple principle and you'll just waste your time. However, this doesn't mean that you shouldn't be original. In fact, you are supposed to make every effort to stick out from your competition while remaining within the imagined realm of the defined culture.

Take some time and find the first few posts of some fresh-made famous brand or influencer. You'll see that those original messages didn't trigger much interest. It was more about feeling the pulse. Later, after gathering intel from analytics, messages started taking shape of something catchy and exciting. The engagement rate suddenly explodes. It finally hit the spot. And that's the breaking moment where some build fortune overnight while others fail to cash in. The reason for such an illogical failure lies in the final rule.

Number three: **you got to sell them something!**

If there's no central or underlying product or service, there is no money. Remember that. All that work to build a giant base of followers won't be enough to even put food on the table if you don't have something to sell. After a while, they will start asking themselves, what the hell are we doing here? What's the point of all of this?

Don't forget that we are living in a consumer society and that deep down we are always expecting a sale. If there's nothing to buy, we turn our attention in another direction. Simple as that.

But **how do you a) stack and b) deliver your products?**

For this, I highly recommend JustOneDime for Amazon FBA online business.

Seth and his expert coaches will teach you how to build a passive income on Amazon. I joined their Amazon FBA Mastery program and found it to be the best course available online. Thanks to them, I'm running a highly profitable online business after trying out a myriad of available options. And while every one of them did return the profit, this feels most comfortable.

In case you are wondering, Amazon FBA stands for Fulfillment by Amazon where you store your inventory in Amazon's centers and they handle everything from there; even providing customer service. That simply means that you don't have to worry about logistics.

However, you do need to learn the secrets of this trade and Seth provides just that.

REMOVING THE LAST OBSTACLE

After reading all of this, you are now confused. And that's okay. It's exactly how you are supposed to feel. So what we're gonna do now is clear the image.

The first thing you need to remember is that none of this will do you any good if you don't step out from the realm of daydreaming and make it happen. As we said, your *have to* must turn into *I need to* or *I must*.

The second thing we are both well-aware of is that you'll most likely opt-in for an online business since it requires less money and time to launch it.

Here, we're going to assume that you are not that crazy about spending ten hours every day for the next couple of months to build a YouTube channel with a sizeable number of followers. Instead, you are more into getting things running ASAP. And I can correlate with that because I'm doing the same thing.

With that in mind, we are left with two choices:

1) Franchising
2) Social Media Marketing

Although, these two don't necessarily cancel each other out. In fact, even if you choose some franchise, you are still required to run online marketing campaigns and they are predominantly done via social networks.

So when you sum everything up, maybe the best course of action should simply be selling online using social media as the primary sales channel. One way or another, you're gonna do SMM so why not cutting short and start making a profit in the next couple of days?

With Amazon FBA as a partner, you are certain that your future customers will get their product as fastest as humanly possible. But that's not the only reason why I'm focusing on Amazon. The other is what we are going through right now.

You see, a dropshipping business really took off in the last couple of years. And now, it's breaking down all over the world. Why? Because the majority of all online dropshipping businesses rely on China to manufacture and ship their products. With the global lockdown caused by the virus outbreak, their businesses are as good as dead.

Even in the best conditions, it sometimes takes over a month for the customer to receive the purchased product. That doesn't reflect well on the brand image, as you can imagine.

With Amazon, these issues don't exist. And that's why I recommended Amazon FBA and Seth and his JustOneDime as the first stop in your future endeavor.

Last but not the least, if you enjoyed reading this, please leave a review on Amazon. First of all, I read every review. Second and more important, reviews help new readers a) discover my books, and b) decide whether or not the subject is interesting to them. Thanks!

www.ingramcontent.com/pod-product-compliance
Lightning Source LLC
Chambersburg PA
CBHW030540220526
45463CB00007B/2910